I0235666

IMAGES
of Rail

Rails of California's Central Coast

ON THE COVER: A black, red, and orange streamlined Southern Pacific Daylight steam locomotive returns to the Central Coast. No. 4449 passes at speed under the Highway 227 bridge south of San Luis Obispo on May 13, 1981. Daylight General Service steam engines were regarded as the "most beautiful locomotive in the world." During their era of service from 1937 to the mid-1950s, the public saw them as the symbol of Central Coast railroading. (Walter Rice photograph.)

IMAGES
of Rail

RAILS OF CALIFORNIA'S CENTRAL COAST

Walter Rice and Emiliano Echeverria

ARCADIA
PUBLISHING

Copyright © 2008 by Walter Rice an Emiliano Echeverria
ISBN 978-1-5316-3552-7

Published by Arcadia Publishing
Charleston, South Carolina

Library of Congress Catalog Card Number: 2007933019

For all general information contact Arcadia Publishing at:
Telephone 843-853-2070
Fax 843-853-0044
E-mail sales@arcadiapublishing.com
For customer service and orders:
Toll-Free 1-888-313-2665

Visit us on the Internet at www.arcadiapublishing.com

A lone suitcase waits to be transferred to the baggage car. With it, the fired-up No. 1330 will shortly begin another passenger train journey from Pacific Grove to San Francisco around 1905. (Randolph Brant collection.)

CONTENTS

Acknowledgments   6

Introduction   7

1.   Streetcar Days of Santa Cruz: Union Traction   11

2.   Sun, Beaches, and Redwood Forests:
     Rails of Santa Cruz County   31

3.   Sugar and Sand: Salinas, Monterey, and Way Stations   51

4.   Steamships, Steam Engines, and Electric Trains:
     Pacific Coast Railway   69

5.   The Coast Line: Connecting the Central Coast   87

Bibliography   127

ACKNOWLEDGMENTS

Many essential individuals who made this volume a reality are unknown. They are the enterprising photographers of a century ago or more who created many of the images we enjoy today. Their names have been lost. However, their work has been saved often by the collector. The genesis of this project began with one such collector: Randolph "Rudy" Brant. Rudy, a Santa Cruz native, was a consummate collector of California steam and street railway photography. His collection has since been passed to coauthor Emiliano Echeverria; its existence directly led the authors to write this book.

Rudy's collection has been blended with other principal collections. Jack Neville's and Chris Stark's outstanding efforts provided, with permission, the end-of-steam-era photography of Art Laidlaw, a retired San Luis Obispo–based Southern Pacific locomotive engineer. Our generous and dear friend Art Lloyd enthusiastically opened his rich photograph collection of Southern Pacific and Pacific Coast Railway steam excursions. The late Art Stump chronicled the end of the Pacific Coast Railway. Roy Christian provided important and meaningful contemporary and historic scenes. Transportation historian and cable car gripman Val Lupiz enriched this work through his search of the San Francisco Public Library newspaper files for Southern Pacific advertisements. Karl Hovanitz, Joe Thompson, and Bruce Battles gave insightful comments about the text.

Some of the more contemporary photography is credited to coauthor Walter Rice. Walter would like to thank his friend Rich Harris for taking him in 1976 to buy his first camera of consequence, and on his official shoot of the Coast Starlight.

We would be remiss if we did not acknowledge the Depression-era management of the Southern Pacific Railroad for defying the conventional wisdom of many of the era by investing the company's very limited resources in creating the "World's Most Beautiful Train."

Our Arcadia editor, Devon Weston, has been constructive, supportive, and encouraging. She is appreciated.

As always, our thanks and gratitude go to all.

Walter Rice, Ph.D.
San Luis Obispo, CA

Emiliano Echeverria
Oakland, CA

INTRODUCTION

The dominant force behind the rail development of California's Central Coast—Santa Cruz, Monterey, and San Luis Obispo Counties—was the San Francisco–based Southern Pacific Railroad. Starting in the 1860s, as the Southern Pacific (SP) progressed south from San Jose, independent railroads that management regarded as having economic potential, such as the Santa Cruz Railroad's 21-mile Watsonville (Pajaro) Santa Cruz line, were eventually incorporated into the Southern Pacific. Rail lines that were regarded as marginal to useless were allowed to survive; the natural economic forces would dispose of such entities. San Luis Obispo's 76-mile Pacific Coast Railway was an example of a marginal entity. The basic long-standing policy of the SP was to buy out or otherwise eliminate effective competition.

As a result of the Southern Pacific constructing south and into Santa Cruz, Monterey, and San Luis Obispo Counties, the flow of commerce changed from surface rail to steamship to exclusively surface rail. Four railroads relied on water transport. The Pacific Coast Railway, Pajaro Valley Consolidated Railroad, Watsonville Transportation Company, and the Santa Cruz and Felton all had deepwater port terminals. For both cargo and traveler, the standard-gauge SP, with its direct access to all of California and the nation, easily economically mastered the narrow-gauge trains with boat connections.

Only the Santa Cruz and Felton was integrated into the SP, and then as a standard-gauge line. It was coupled with the Southern Pacific's purchase and subsequent conversion to standard gauge of the South Pacific Coast Railroad, which ran from the east side of San Francisco Bay south to San Jose, then on to Los Gatos and through the timber-rich Santa Cruz Mountains to Felton. Through this acquisition, the SP had a second route to Santa Cruz.

The Southern Pacific's Santa Cruz County trackage was concluded with the acquisition of what would become known as the Davenport Branch. In 1907, the Coast Line Railroad Company completed the 11.9 miles of track between Santa Cruz and Davenport, the site of the Portland Cement plant. The track was deeded in 1917 to the SP, which had operated the line.

The SP was in fact the second railroad to complete a line from Santa Cruz to Davenport. The Ocean Shore Railway's first revenue train ran from Santa Cruz to Swanton—north of Davenport—on May 16, 1906. The grand design of the Ocean Shore was to build an electric railway from San Francisco to Santa Cruz via the Pacific Ocean shoreline. Except for 2.4 miles of San Francisco electrification, the Ocean Shore was a steam railway that was in two parts—northern and southern sections with a gap between served by a Stanley Steamer. The Ocean Shore ceased in October 1920. The Davenport Branch, however, is still in service.

A comparable history of railway development to that of Santa Cruz County occurred for the Monterey Peninsula. The 3-foot-gauge Monterey and Salinas Valley Railroad Company opened for service in October 1874 between Castroville (Del Monte Junction) and Monterey. At a foreclosure sale in December 1879, the firm was acquired by the Pacific Improvement Company, a subsidiary of the Southern Pacific. The new owners converted the line to standard-gauge trackage. During March 1888, it was consolidated with the SP. Also under construction during this period was the San Luis Obispo–based narrow-gauge Pacific Coast Railway. Please refer to chapter four for details.

Santa Cruz's Union Traction Company and Monterey and Pacific Grove streetcar systems held no interest for the SP, since they lacked freight potential. Their passenger base was also weak.

Curiously, the May 5, 1894, arrival (from the north) of the SP in San Luis Obispo sent the San Luis Street Railway horsecar service out of business. The new SP depot was close to the city's population center, whereas the Pacific Coast Railway's station was at a distance. Citizens soon discovered they could easily walk such short trips as an alternative to using the generally inconvenient and slow (speeds ranged between four and six miles per hour) horsecar service.

In 1901, the SP was immortalized in Frank Norris's classic muckraking book *The Octopus*. The term *Octopus* soon became a nickname for the Southern Pacific, as the company became infamous for its ruthless predatory tactics. Freight rates were often adjusted upward when eastern market prices for California's agriculture increased. However, the large, essentially privately funded capital investment in right-of-way, track, equipment, and other components of infrastructure to bring the railway to the Central Coast stimulated economic development. Agriculture from the land-locked Salinas Valley communities now could get to market. Common tourists could easily holiday at Santa Cruz's casino and boardwalk and the wealthy at Monterey's Del Monte Hotel, "the Newport of the Western Continent."

If the Southern Pacific had exercised its power in a ruthless fashion during the late 19th and early 20th centuries, the company behaved admirably during the Great Depression. In late 1935, during the trough of America's greatest economic collapse, SP executives began formulating plans for a new streamlined train to be powered by the best steam locomotives in the world.

The result debuted on March 21, 1937. The black, red, and orange Daylight passenger train began operating on a fast nine-and-three-quarter-hour Coast Line schedule between San Francisco and Los Angeles. On August 4, the new train carried its 100,000th passenger in the shortest time ever for an American passenger train. Streamlined and powerful Golden State (later called General Service) locomotives pulled the Daylight at speeds as high as 79 miles per hour. These powerful GS locomotives' range allowed them to run the entire distance from San Francisco to Los Angeles—a world's distance record for a single locomotive. Fares were slashed, too, by about two-thirds when evaluated against the fares of the 1920s. The "World's Most Beautiful Train" proved highly profitable.

The Daylight, coupled with the all-sleeper overnight Lark, captured the public's imagination. The once-detested Southern Pacific was enjoying the zenith of public approval. Its Daylight trains, run with precision, soon became a symbol of California.

Choosing the cover image for this volume was easy. If one photograph had to be selected, what could be more representative of Central Coast rails than a GS locomotive resplendent in its black, red, and orange colors?

Times and management are, however, subject to change. Freeways and airplanes began to erode passenger train ridership. Trucking was siphoning off both less-than-carload freight and short-haul freight movements. The SP management of the 1960s reacted to these external forces by engaging in tactics designed to drive away the remaining customers in these categories. Passenger trains and services were thus eliminated and downgraded.

In 1971, when Amtrak took over most of America's intercity passenger trains, only two SP Central Coast intercity trains were left: the Del Monte and the Daylight. The While the Del Monte was discontinued, the Daylight was restructured by Amtrak to run from Los Angeles to Oakland four days a week and San Diego to Seattle tri-weekly. This evolved into a daily Los Angeles–Seattle service under the Coast Starlight name.

The Southern Pacific's level freight service became infamous to the delight of competitors. Salinas Valley agricultural shippers, for example, found it economically desirable to truck their shipments to Stockton to ship east via the Union Pacific rather than use the SP from Salinas. The railroad's corporate culture was in a downward spiral. The end came in 1996, when the SP became but another railroad folded into the Union Pacific. The once-powerful Octopus was no more.

Thanks to government investments—federal, state, and local—combined with investment by the Union Pacific, Coast Line passenger operations have expanded and long freight trains again characterize line.

It is now time to ride the rails of the Central Coast. All aboard!

What was the delight of San Francisco's World's Fair in 1915, miniature, 19-inch-gague, Pacific-type locomotives are still operating today (2008) on the Swanton Pacific Railroad on Santa Cruz County's north coast. Engine No. 1914 is getting water at Swanton, July 1999. (Walter Rice photograph.)

No one is buying sweets today at the Orchid Sweet Shop, as No. 18 has spectacularly blocked its entrance. Beach-bound Car No. 30 waits to gain clearance around the crowd. A rebuilt No.18 was in fact the last non-Birney car in service at the time of the January 1926 closure. (Randolph Brant collection.)

One

STREETCAR DAYS OF SANTA CRUZ
UNION TRACTION

Streetcars left the streets of Santa Cruz at the early date of January 15, 1926, when the last car of the Union Traction Company rolled into the Pacific Avenue carbarn shortly after midnight. The increasing use of the automobile was producing a gradual but substantial decline in ridership. Resulting revenues were inadequate to maintain the system. Further, significant capital investment to rebuild the company's rundown infrastructure had to be made if streetcar service was to continue. The company's four modern Birney cars, purchased in 1922, were hampered in their operation by the condition of the roadbed. All of this resulted in management's logical shift to the more economical Mack motor coaches.

A 1904 consolidation created the Union Traction Company from two narrow-gauge companies: the Santa Cruz, Capitola, and Watsonville Railway and the Santa Cruz Electric Railway. The Santa Cruz, Capitola, and Watsonville, which had electrified by 1903, was the successor to the East Santa Cruz Street Railway, a horsecar company. The Santa Cruz Electric could trace its ancestry back to the city's first electrification in 1891.

On July 7, 1906, ownership of the Union Traction passed to the Coast Counties Power Company and the leadership of John Martin, cofounder of the Pacific Gas and Electric Company. Under Martin, the company was converted to standard gauge with passing sidings (1907)—except downtown, where it was double-tracked—and the Laveaga Park branch was built (1908–1910). Union Traction thus evolved into three main lines: Ocean Cliffs via Mission Street, Seabright-Capitola, and Laveaga Park via Water Street. All lines including short turns terminated at Santa Cruz's Beach Casino, the company's major summer traffic generator. The exception was the Seabright-Capitola service, which ended downtown at Soquel and Pacific Avenues.

The company started standard-gauge service in September 1907 with five California-style cars (open-end sections with an enclosed center section) built in the shops of the Sacramento Gas and Electric Company. By July 1908, the company's fleet had reached 19 with an additional 14 cars, many of which were former narrow-gauge cars reconstructed in the company's shops. All cars required two men—a motorman and a conductor—until immediately after World War I, when the fleet was converted to one-man operation. Most of these cars were scrapped by 1924.

In April 1922, Union Traction purchased four Birney Safety cars against the advice of the California Railroad Commission, which felt the company's tracks were in too poor condition for the single-truck Birney cars. These cars provided service until closure.

Like most cities, Santa Cruz's first rail service was via horsecar. As beachgoers stroll along the boardwalk in suits and long dresses, reflecting the bygone era of the 1890s, Pacific Avenue Street Railroad Company horsecar Nos. 2 and 5 head toward the center of Santa Cruz. Behind the horsecars is the standard-gauge track of the Southern Pacific Railroad. (Randolph Brant collection.)

East Santa Cruz Horse Railroad closed car No. 4 sits at Soquel Road in 1894. The car's front dash is thick with mud from the four-legged motive power. The company had a unique gauge of 3 feet 2.25 inches. (Randolph Brant collection.)

Undoubtedly, those posed on East Santa Cruz Horse Railroad No. 1 about 1880 were important community members or company men. The location is near the carbarn at Soquel Road and Doyle. The leftward-leading track goes to the carbarn. (Walter Rice collection.)

The East Santa Cruz Horse Railroad connected Santa Cruz's downtown Lower Plaza with places east of the San Lorenzo River like Soquel Road, Arana Gulch, East Cliff, and Twin Lakes. The single patron on open car No. 2 is not generating sufficient revenue to keep the horse in feed. (Randolph Brant collection.)

Beachgoers rapidly alight at the beach attraction Tent City, which offered private tent rentals and a restaurant. Santa Cruz Electric open car No. 6 was constructed in 1892. Tent City had its own short spur on the north. (Randolph Brant collection.)

Here an open-bench Santa Cruz Electric car carries an overflow load that surely put a smile on the face of the company's treasurer. The Bedell House was an upscale Mission Street hotel. Next to the boardwalk are the tracks of the Santa Cruz, Capitola, and Watsonville, and in the middle are those of the standard-gauge Southern Pacific. (Randolph Brant collection.)

Brand-new Santa Cruz, Capitola, and Watsonville No. 11, a 1903 product of the St. Louis Car Company, has started another journey to Capitola in the late summer of 1903. A year later, this beach scene would be transformed as Santa Cruz's major beach icon, the Casino building, would replace the undistinguished wooden structures. (Randolph Brant collection.)

Cars of the two independent companies that would create Union Traction pass in front of the imposing Sea Beach Hotel before their 1904 consolidation. Car No. 13 of the Santa Cruz, Capitola, and Watsonville is in the foreground, while No. 5 of the Santa Cruz, Garfield Park, and Capitola (Santa Cruz Electric) is on the far side of the Southern Pacific tracks. (Randolph Brant collection.)

During September 1904, Santa Cruz's new palace, the magnificent Casino, is thriving with pleasure seekers as No. 11 heads toward its new terminal on the north side of the city's most important edifice. Previously, cars of the Santa Cruz, Capitola, and Watsonville ended on the beach or the south side of the amusement structures. (Randolph Brant collection.)

On December 29, 1903, a Santa Cruz, Capitola, and Watsonville single-truck California-style car hosted a Grand Excursion to Capitola for the benefit of furnishing the free library. No. 9's charitable "lady conductors" have stopped for a photograph at East Twin Lakes. (Randolph Brant collection.)

Two companies' bridges competing for local traffic over the Soquel River are pictured here. In the foreground is the Santa Cruz, Capitola, and Watsonville electric streetcar line that lead into Capitola's city center. The bridge in the background is that of the Southern Pacific Railroad as part of their Santa Cruz branch. Note the formal dress of these boating ladies reflecting a different era. (Randolph Brant collection.)

This view from Opal Heights shows the electric line's entry to Capitola over the Soquel River. Service directly into Capitola began in late 1903. The Santa Cruz, Capitola, and Watsonville Railway Company's grandiose corporate title proved to be beyond the scope of economic reality. Watsonville was an impossible goal. (Randolph Brant collection.)

Although still bearing its former company markings, Capitola car No. 14 is in Union Traction service at Santa Cruz Beach's Tent City. Since October 29, 1904, Capitola cars have traveled the northernmost beachfront tracks, formerly only used by Santa Cruz Electric cars. (Randolph Brant collection.)

Now under the ownership of Union Traction, former Santa Cruz Electric Railway car No. 4, an 1891 product of Stockton, unloads properly dressed pleasure goers at the beach's Tent City spur in 1905. The fate of the narrow-gauge fleet is unknown after the September 1907 conversion to standard gauge. (Randolph Brant collection.)

18

The standard-gauge era is modeled by California-style car No. 5, a 1907 product of the Sacramento Gas and Electric shops. Car Nos. 1 to 5 featured a unique manual rope braking system and rebuilt archbar trucks from Southern Pacific freight cars. No. 5 appears at Vue dé l'eau trolley station at the end of the Ocean Cliff line. (Randolph Brant collection.)

As delivered from Sacramento Gas and Electric, car No. 5 had an open center section with crosswise seating. Outbound from the beach during off-season in 1908, No. 5 passes the early-20th-century classic resort hotel the Sea Beach, which was totally destroyed by fire in June 1912. (Randolph Brant collection.)

The two-man car operation is the still the standard of Union Traction, as witnessed by this photograph of a posed motorman and conductor in front of car No. 14. A typical practice of the period was for commercial photographers to pose streetcar crews and then return a few days later to sell to the crew their portraits. (Randolph Brant collection.)

At the Southern Pacific crossing and station at Seabright Avenue, car No. 14 awaits departure time for another trip to downtown Santa Cruz in 1912. Seabright service was in reality a short-turn city service of the Capitola interurban line. (Randolph Brant collection.)

It is "BASE BALL" today. What would be more fun: a ride on open double-truck car No. 30 (of unknown origin) or the old ball game? Would you care "if you never got back" if No. 30 waited to carry you home? (Randolph Brant collection.)

With the 1911 opening of the Casa Del Rey Hotel, car No. 20 was permanently assigned to transfer guests between the hotel and the Southern Pacific depot. No. 20 was originally built as a cable car for San Francisco's Omnibus Company and later rebuilt by the Market Street Railway (of 1893) as a single-truck California-type electric car, known locally as a "dinky." (Randolph Brant collection.)

Sacramento Gas and Electric–built car No. 3 is stopped just beyond the Municipal Pier. The closed pier restaurant and lack of beachgoers clearly imply it is winter. An unidentified motorman has his portrait taken at the controls of No. 3. He has provided an excellent view of the end construction details of the Sacramento cars. (Randolph Brant collection.)

The atmosphere of Santa Cruz's main business artery is captured in this classic 1913 photograph. Looking north on Pacific Avenue, the view shows Union Traction car No. 17. At Soquel Avenue (right), No. 12 waits to leave for either Seabright or Capitola. The automobile age has yet to arrive. (Randolph Brant collection.)

From 1907 to 1915, many Santa Cruz Beachgoers enjoyed a trip from the Casino along the boardwalk on the Bay Shore Limited, which was powered by a 22-inch-gauge steam engine, an early-20th-century creation. After multiple near-misses of the scrapper, the engine, now known as "Little Puffer," ran at the Fleishhacker Zoo from 1925 to 1978. In 1998, this historic miniature steam train began a second career at the San Francisco Zoo, where it can be ridden today. (Roy Christian collection.)

Under the ownership of the Coast Counties Power Company, Union Traction extended trackage to Santa Cruz's Laveaga Park. In this c. 1910 scene, Santa Cruz is in the distance, having yet to grow to the park. Car No. 17, running in undeveloped territory, approaches the terminus with another load of park hikers. (Randolph Brant collection.)

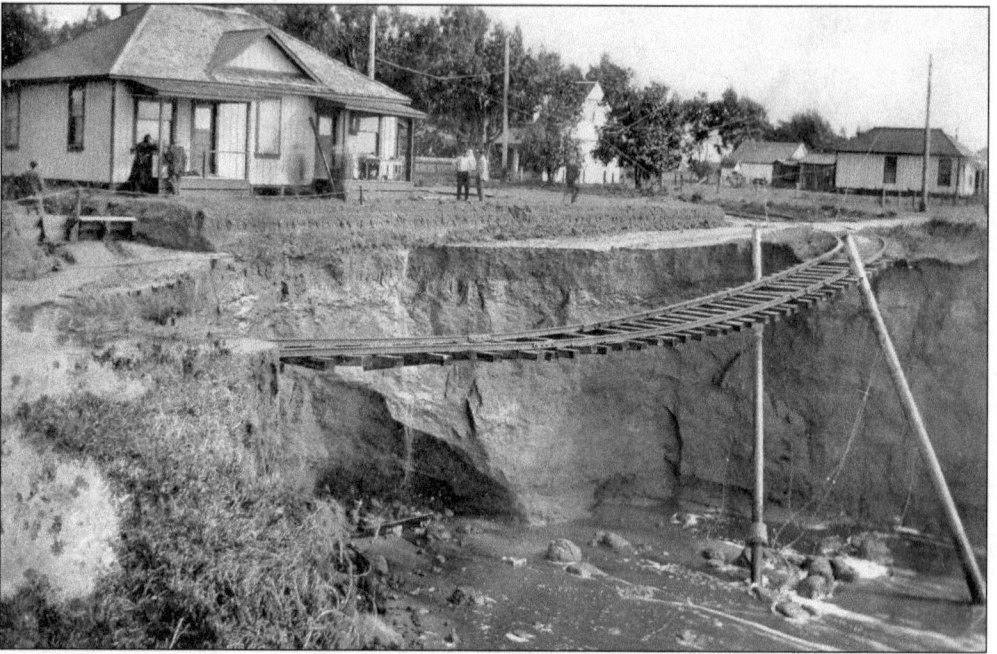

Before the heavy rains of the winter of 1912, the tracks—suspended in mid-air—rested on the washed-away Twin Lakes Trestle, which curved into Twelfth Avenue. Capitola was without service. To Union Traction's credit, the company soon had crews driving piles for a replacement bridge. (Randolph Brant collection.)

A St. Louis Car Company product, No. 18 lays over in front of the 160-room Hotel Capitola, the eastern terminus of the Union Traction and its predecessor, the Santa Cruz, Capitola, and Watsonville. The locals who organized the original company were a front for Chicago utility magnate H. M. Byllesby. The Byllesby Company would later operate San Francisco's Market Street Railway from 1925 to 1938. (Randolph Brant collection.)

A one-man inbound Seabright car crosses the San Lorenzo River to enter downtown Santa Cruz while the new concrete span is being built in 1920. Passengers wishing to go to the "Band Concert—Beach" had to transfer at Pacific Avenue to a beach-bound car, as Seabright and Capitola cars terminated at the city center. (Randolph Brant collection.)

At the east end of the San Lorenzo River Bridge, outbound Capitola car No. 18 struck and overturned an automobile on August 25, 1921. While its one-man crew and most of its passengers were aiding the victims, No. 18 started rolling back at speed toward town. Rounding the corner onto Pacific, No. 18 toppled on its side. Note that the former Southern Pacific freight car archbar trucks remained upright. (Randolph Brant collection.)

One-man car No. 11 is inbound on Pacific Avenue, heading toward the Southern Pacific depot and the beach, either from the Ocean Cliff or Laveaga Park line in 1920. Since August 1918, passengers have paid 6¢ instead of the customary nickel. (Randolph Brant collection.)

In this c. 1906 view of Union Traction's Pacific Avenue carbarn, the tracks are still narrow gauge and Sycamore Street has yet to be paved. Seen in the barn are No. 4, signed up for the Bedell House shuttle service, and a wooden tower car. (Randolph Brant collection.)

In 1922, Union Traction purchased four Birney Safety cars, Nos. 21 to 24, from the American Car Company for $25,252. The Birneys ran the majority of service, as the level of operations was drastically being reduced. Here No. 22 is shown at the beach with the Casino in the background. No. 22 will soon make an Ocean Cliffs schedule, by far the company's busiest line. (Randolph Brant collection.)

Birney No. 23 has completed its last Laveaga Park streetcar run, and Mack bus No. 1 is posed next to it to illustrate the old and new on December 8, 1925. The political importance of the

occasion is exemplified by Mayor John Maher's presence in front of No. 23. The four Birney cars would be sold to Bakersfield. (Randolph Brant collection.)

4TH OF JULY
and every Sunday
EXCURSIONS

SACRAMENTO STOCKTON
$1.25
ROUNDTRIP

Same roundtrip fare to Davis, Woodland, Tracy, Lodi, etc.

SAN JOSE
$1 ROUNDTRIP

SANTA CRUZ
$1.25
ROUNDTRIP
on the "Sun Tan Special"

The "Sun Tan" leaves San Francisco (Third St.) 7:55 a.m. every Sunday and holiday, arriving Santa Cruz Beach 10:35 a.m. RETURNING, leaves Santa Cruz 5:45 p.m., arrives San Francisco 8:25 p.m.

FIREWORKS, JULY 4—Biggest and most spectacular display ever attempted at Santa Cruz. SPECIAL TRAIN for San Francisco leaves after the fireworks.

FROM OAKLAND, "East Bay Sun Tan" direct to Santa Cruz every Sunday and holiday.

$2 ROUNDTRIP if you go down Saturdays or July 3, return following day.

To all other points Southern Pacific's regular fares are 2¢ a mile and less. Avoid crowded highways—let the engineer do the driving! Take the whole family. Children from 5 to 11, half fare; under 5, free.

Southern Pacific

For any other fares or passenger information, phone DOuglas 1255.
(Other railway business, DOuglas 1212.)

It is time to flee the summer fog of San Francisco and enjoy the beach, surf, and boardwalk of Santa Cruz via the Suntan Special, for a round-trip price of only $1.25. San Franciscans would board the Special at 7:55 a.m. and return to the city's Third and Townsend Southern Pacific depot at 8:33 p.m. (Val Lupiz collection.)

Two

SUN, BEACHES, AND REDWOOD FORESTS
RAILS OF SANTA CRUZ COUNTY

Of California's counties, only San Francisco is physically smaller than Santa Cruz County. Despite the area being rich in lumber, the state's most powerful railroad—the Southern Pacific—declined in the early 1870s to build a line from its railhead at Pajaro (Watsonville) to Santa Cruz. This forced local businessmen to organize, build, and open the 21-mile 3-foot-gauge Santa Cruz Railroad. At the same time, the 7-mile narrow-gauge Santa Cruz and Felton opened primarily to carry lumber to connecting steamships.

The 3-foot-gauge South Pacific Coast Railroad was the most ambitious railroad plan, whose route ran from the east side of San Francisco Bay south to San Jose, then on to Los Gatos and through the Santa Cruz Mountains to Felton. To bridge the mountains, eight tunnels were required, two of which were greater than 5,000 feet. By 1887, all three of these lines had fallen to Southern Pacific control and were converted to standard gauge.

Southern Pacific completed its Santa Cruz County trackage in 1917, when it formally absorbed the Coast Line Railroad, which had built north to Davenport to serve the cement plant and to provide a competitive check on what proved to be a failed venture: the Ocean Shore Railroad. The Ocean Shore also had coastal trackage north from Santa Cruz.

At its zenith around 1918, there were 18 passenger and 6 freight trains a day arriving in and departing from Santa Cruz. Today the Union Pacific Railroad operates freight trains from Watsonville Junction to Davenport, and the Santa Cruz, Big Trees, and Pacific Railway—a diesel-powered tourist and common carrier operation—runs between Santa Cruz and Felton (Olympia). The Santa Cruz Mountain line ended in 1940 after major washouts.

The enormous stands of virgin timber made Santa Cruz County a center for California's early lumber industry. Small lumber railroads dotted the Santa Cruz Mountains. However, by the start of the 20th century, timber suitable for cutting was all but exhausted. Today the feel of these lumber roads is in part maintained by the Roaring Camp and Big Trees Narrow-Gauge Railroad, which runs from Felton to the top of nearby Bear Mountain, a distance of about two and a half miles. The county's most unique rail operation was at Davenport: Santa Cruz Portland Cement's narrow-gauge electrified plant railroad. Workers and limestone quarry were transported on this private railway. A standard-gauge section employed steam power. Motor vehicles have since replaced the rail.

The Jupiter still exists today. After the Southern Pacific's purchase of the Santa Cruz Railroad, the Jupiter roamed the railway trackage of El Salvador, where it was discovered in the 1960s and eventually placed on display at the Smithsonian. (Randolph Brant collection.)

The 3-foot-gauge Santa Cruz and Felton Railroad ran from 1875 to 1887, when it was taken into the Southern Pacific. In 1906, the company converted the line to standard gauge. A crew poses with a locomotive at the line's Felton depot about 1890 before hauling lumber to the Santa Cruz wharf. (Randolph Brant collection.)

Three-foot narrow-gauge South Pacific Coast trains ran from the Alameda Pier to Felton/Santa Cruz by way of San Jose, Los Gatos, and the Santa Cruz Mountains. From 1876 until July 1, 1887, when the railway was leased to the Southern Pacific, the company was an independent operation. (Randolph Brant collection.)

The white flag on the front of South Pacific Coast engine No. 9 signifies an extra, or nonscheduled train. The crew and passengers of the single-car special pose for the camera. Who is that young pigtailed lass near No. 9's cab, an actress? Is an early version of The Perils of Pauline about to be filmed? Remember that Newark, the South Pacific Coast's home city, had an early motion picture studio. (Randolph Brant collection.)

In 1880, when the South Pacific Coast opened across the Santa Cruz Mountains to Felton, the new area it traversed was rich with enormous stands of virgin timber. It was only natural and economically logical that the road's fuel be wood. No. 13's tender is stacked high with wood that the fireman will soon be placing in the firebox. (Randolph Brant collection.)

Trains of any consequence, such Los Gatos–bound No. 502, required two locomotives to conquer the grades presented by the Santa Cruz Mountains. The narrow-gauge South Pacific Coast Line became standard gauge in 1909. Here young ladies from a mountain summer encampment await an important arrival from Santa Cruz in the 1920s. Management is not pleased, since a single piece of luggage implies only one outbound revenue rider. (Randolph Brant collection.)

A South Pacific Coast train has stopped at Tuxedo (now Mount Herman) to board schoolgirls returning from summer holidays in the Santa Cruz Mountains. (Roy Christian collection.)

The Valencia Mills logging railroad, seen in 1891, was representative of the many logging operations that sprung up in the late 1800s to take advantage of the Santa Cruz Mountains' virgin timber. Many of San Francisco's Victorian houses descended from these timber stands. Since the sole purpose of logging railroads was to haul logs to the mill, their construction and operational standards were minimal. (Randolph Brant collection.)

The Dougherty Lumber Company ran a lumber railroad 8.15 miles to a timber stand from a junction with the South Pacific Coast Railway at Boulder Creek. When the Southern Pacific converted the South Pacific Coast from 3-foot gauge to standard gauge, the lumber line was likewise converted. It was abandoned in 1918. (Randolph Brant collection.)

Judging by the boaters on the Soquel River and the double-headed inbound Santa Cruz passenger train on the Capitola trestle, it is summertime, high season for the railroad. Three baggage cars imply many tourists and, more importantly, a bonanza for local innkeepers. The World War I–era lady boaters are properly dressed for such activity, complete with open parasols to fend off Capitola's sun. (Randolph Brant collection.)

The line is clear, as indicated by the down position of the semaphore signal for the soon-to-be-arriving train bound for Santa Cruz. A photographer with an open tripod set up in front of the luggage cart is ready to record the arrival. Judging from the size of the station, Capitola was not an important stop; nevertheless, it still offered Western Union and Wells Fargo Express services. (Randolph Brant collection.)

It is a hot day in Santa Cruz, as evidenced by the open coach windows in this 1930s photograph. The train has just departed Santa Cruz's famous boardwalk. Perhaps the coaches overheated sunning themselves in the yard. Once the San Lorenzo River Bridge has been cleared, the next stop will be Seabright. (Randolph Brant collection.)

During the heyday of Southern Pacific's Santa Cruz passenger and freight train service, about 1918, the Santa Cruz yard is deep and rich with cars and activity. Soon another passenger local will leave the depot and make the short trip to the Casino for beachgoers and then head on to Watsonville Junction before its arrival at the citadel of west San Francisco. (Randolph Brant collection.)

Trains such as this passenger local were reversed by means of a wye at Santa Cruz. They would head up the northbound left-hand track with the engine in the lead. Then they would back across the top of the wye and onto the right-hand track. The engine, now on the opposite end of the train, was ready to proceed to the Casino, way stations, and Watsonville Junction. (Randolph Brant collection.)

Labor-intensive steam passenger trains were (and are) expensive to run, requiring relatively heavy passenger counts for their economic justification. Where such counts were impossible, the SP sometimes turned to wind-dynamic McKeen motor cars, such as No. 31, pictured at Ben Lomond. Buck Rogers of the 25th century would be right at home piloting a McKeen car. The more permanent solution was outright abandonment, often with a Greyhound bus replacement. (Randolph Brant collection.)

On April 25, 1948, Southern Pacific excursion goers enjoy the redwoods of the Santa Cruz Mountains and undoubtedly a bucolic picnic as the train lays over at Felton, approximately eight miles from the Casino. The trackage between Santa Cruz and Felton was once part of the South Pacific Coast Railroad; since 1985, it has been operated by the Santa Cruz, Big Trees, and Pacific Railway, a diesel-powered tourist and common carrier operation. (Art Lloyd photograph.)

Following several days of turbulent storms, on the afternoon of February 26, 1940, the Los Gatos–Santa Cruz line was permanently closed by mudslides and washouts between the small community of Olympia and Los Gatos. This rare 1948 jaunt has reached the Olympia end of track, 8.8 miles north of Santa Cruz. (Art Lloyd photograph.)

It is now time to travel from Davenport back to Santa Cruz and up the Coast Line to San Francisco on April 25, 1948. This double-header, consisting of Nos. 2374 and 2915, has been wyed. Soon locomotives will couple onto the former rear of the train, the new front. A brakeman operates the switch to make this a reality. (Art Lloyd photograph.)

The Southern Pacific's Santa Cruz operation ran on city streets, the most famous of which was along the beachfront. Engine Nos. 2915 and 2374, returning on an inbound excursion from Felton in 1948, have begun traveling on a residential street. No. 2915 rings its bell to warn innocent motorists. (Wilbur C. Whittaker photograph.)

The most spectacular part of the Watsonville Junction/Santa Cruz line is the Soquel River (or Capitola) trestle. The town of Capitola-by-the-Sea's downtown lies underneath the trestle. A Suntan Special has reached near midpoint on the trestle in April 1948. (Art Lloyd photograph.)

In 1940, washouts ended the former South Pacific Coast line via the Santa Cruz Mountains and its giant redwoods. Santa Cruz trains were then routed via the Coast Line to Watsonville Junction, where they branched off following the right-of-way of what once was the Santa Cruz Railroad. This excursion train has reached the junction in July 1951. (Art Lloyd photograph.)

Environmentalists shudder when viewing this photograph, but contemporary rail fans were more than delighted by this magnificent (but wasteful) display of smoke near Capitola in July 1951. Thank you, Southern Pacific. (Art Lloyd photograph.)

For working-class San Franciscans, *Santa Cruz* spelled a day of pleasure. Southern Pacific accommodated this desire with both scheduled and excursion trains. Soon these excursionists will exit their San Francisco commuter coaches to enjoy the pleasures of the beach and boardwalk in 1952. (Art Lloyd photograph.)

A double-header steam set led by No. 2517 (built by Schenectady in 1901) cautiously makes its way down Santa Cruz's Beach Street to the Casino stop, where hundreds of beachgoers will board, in 1949. Unlike their motorized brethren, these people did not experience the hassle of hunting for a parking place. (Art Lloyd photograph.)

Santa Cruz beach traffic is heavy. SP No. 2517 and its mate haul an extra section of today's Suntan Special, the Southern Pacific's mild-season weekend train, in 1950. While the weekenders enjoy themselves, their train rests in the Santa Cruz yard. (Art Lloyd photograph.)

In this April 25, 1948, view, a double-header excursion train led by No. 2916 (built by Schenectady in 1898) has just left the Santa Cruz yards. It will soon arrive at the landmark of the city's beach: the Casino. Here the exhausted crowds typically flock onto the train to return to San Francisco. (Art Lloyd photograph.)

44

Traveling along the coast of Capitola in July 1951 is one of many steam excursions sponsored by the Pacific Coast chapter of the Railway Locomotive Historical Society, under the direction of Art Lloyd. The excursion could pass for a Suntan Special, as it runs along the former right-of-way of the long-forgotten Santa Cruz Railroad. (Art Lloyd photograph.)

Besides the Felton (Olympia) branch from Santa Cruz, the approximately nine-mile-long northward branch to Davenport traveled along what was mostly windswept, barren ocean shore. This 1948 excursion train has stopped so rail fans can record on film the passage of the train over an ocean-hugging trestle. (Art Lloyd photograph.)

Ocean Shore No. 3 pulls freight near Davenport. No. 3, a classic 10-wheeler, was built in 1881 by Schenectady. A former Southern Pacific locomotive, it was acquired by the Ocean Shore in 1906 and scrapped nine years later. (Randolph Brant collection.)

This south end Ocean Shore passenger train will soon leave Santa Cruz for a shoreline journey to Swanton, where passengers will board a Stanley Steamer stage to connect with north end trains at Tunitas. A distance of over 80 miles will be covered before Santa Cruz–boarding passengers will arrive in San Francisco. The trip will be breathtaking and spectacular, but not time-competitive to Southern Pacific's Santa Cruz schedules. (Randolph Brant collection.)

A south end Ocean Shore crew poses in front of a passenger local at Swanton. Service ran between Swanton and Santa Cruz from 1906 to 1920, when most of the southern district trackage was sold to the San Vincent Lumber Company. The lumber company could then boast 14.4 miles of line. The success was short lived, as the railroad was abandoned three years later in 1923. (Randolph Brant collection.)

Before conversion to trucking, the Santa Cruz Cement Company at Davenport operated a 3-foot-gauge electrified railroad to haul rock from the quarry. In 1924, crew and plant employees stand in front of a quarry train, which is being pulled by an 18-ton 0-4-0 Baldwin-built locomotive with a mining-type engine. The line's rail was 60-pound, with 600 volts of DC power collected by trolley. (Randolph Brant collection.)

In 1942, the Santa Cruz Cement Company purchased a unique streetcar for it employees. Much altered and streamlined, the car was built from the remains of the Pacific Coast Railway's Santa Maria–Guadalupe Interurban car No. 3 (see chapter four). (Randolph Brant collection.)

During the heyday of electric operation, the yards of the Santa Cruz Portland Company at Davenport clearly suggest a scale that is intense. Very few industries merit their own mainline railroad branch. (Roy Christian collection.)

Southern Pacific continued its Santa Cruz–Davenport passenger service after the Ocean Shore's creditors forced abandonment. As illustrated by this single-car train, the operation did not endear itself to the railroad's accounting department. The justification for the Davenport branch—then and now—is the freight revenues generated by the Portland Cement plant. (Randolph Brant collection.)

Pictured at Seabright is switcher No. 1235, one of a group of 15 switchers the Southern Pacific received from Baldwin in 1915. The level of local freight activity even at the end of the steam era required the railroad to use a switch engine to spot the many freight cars on the appropriate sidings. (Roy Christian collection.)

During 1996, the Union Pacific Railroad absorbed the once-powerful but economically weakened Southern Pacific. Today Santa Cruz's rail freight connection to the nation is by the Union Pacific, as evidenced here. (Roy Christian photograph.)

The first station after the Santa Cruz branch left the Coast Line at Watsonville Junction was Watsonville. Life in most small communities found the local station the hub of community activity, most notably at train time. Even if there was no train, the depot was a point of socialization, which is undoubtedly a prime reason why these boys and men were there. (Randolph Brant collection.)

Three

SUGAR AND SAND
SALINAS, MONTEREY, AND WAY STATIONS

Rail services in the Salinas-Monterey area ranged from the diminutive 3-foot-gauge Salinas Railway Company passenger steam dummy that connected, for a two-year period from 1898 to 1900, Salinas with the giant sugar mill at Spreckels to Southern Pacific's Monterey branch, with its famous Del Monte Limited train. The Monterey branch left the Coast Line at Castroville and connected the Monterey Peninsula—notably Seaside, Fort Ord, Monterey, and Pacific Grove—with the entire country.

The scale of the Spreckels sugar mill was of such proportions that in 1929 the company built three and a half miles of industrial standard-gauge steam trackage to facilitate operations. The Pajaro Valley Railway's 3-foot-gauge lines connected Salinas, Watsonville, and Spreckels with the deepwater seaport of Moss Landing. The August 1, 1929, abandonment of the Pajaro Valley Railway prompted Spreckels into railway construction. The failure of the Pajaro Valley line was due to the economic impracticality of water transport when compared to surface transport.

Although a Santa Cruz County entity, the short-lived Watsonville Transportation was built to compete with the Southern Pacific and the Pajaro Valley Railway for the rich agricultural output of the Pajaro Valley. The company constructed a 3-foot-6-inch electric line from the center of Watsonville to a Monterey Bay wharf. It operated single-car passenger motors and freight trains. The competition and ruinous high seas, which destroyed the line's wharf, caused total abandonment of its final successor in October 1913.

Like the residents of Santa Cruz, the citizens of Monterey and Pacific Grove enjoyed a reasonably extensive local trolley car system: the Monterey and Pacific Grove Railway. In 1890, a 3-foot-gauge horsecar service was provided. Electrification occurred in June 1903, narrow-gauge trackage was converted to standard gauge, and the company's 10 horsecars were motorized for the conversion. An additional nine new electric cars were acquired during 1904–1905 from the St. Louis Car Company, plus the firm built a line to round out its roster.

The Monterey and Pacific Grove Railway connected the Del Monte Hotel, downtown Monterey, and Pacific Grove—including that city's Southern Pacific depot—with residential neighborhoods. World War I brought an influx of new temporary residents and thus record ridership. After the war, most of these temporary residents returned home. Ridership collapsed. The smaller population base, combined with the ever-expanding usage of the automobile, created an economic environment that left management with only a single rational option: total abandonment. This occurred on July 20, 1923.

The Salinas Railway ran for only two years, from 1898 to 1900, connecting Salinas with the Spreckels sugar mill, a distance of 5 miles. The company's steam dummy No. 1 and three-man crew pose at Salinas. After the Pajaro Valley Railroad absorbed this line, No. 1 was sold to the Utah Construction Company, which in turn abandoned the dummy in 1912. (Randolph Brant collection.)

Looking south from Salinas's Main Street on January 7, 1930, this view shows the abandoned (formally since August 1, 1929) freight house and 3-foot-gauge trackage of the Pajaro Valley Consolidated Railroad (PVCRR) on the right. After PVCRR's peak sugar beet–hauling season of 1917, hauls dropped off dramatically as trucks took over the short-haul traffic. After the 1927 season, the engines were stored. On the left is the Southern Pacific's Coast Line. (Randolph Brant collection.)

PVCRR No. 7 (2-6-0), a June 1900 product of the Baldwin Locomotive Works, is on the company's turntable at the road's northern point, Watsonville, around 1920. In 1930, the defunct PVCRR sold its eight remaining steam locomotives to the Southern Pacific, which stored them until 1935, when they were scrapped. (Randolph Brant collection.)

Engine No. 1 (2-4-2T) sits in front of the PVCRR engine house at Spreckels about 1898. No. 1 was built by Baldwin in 1890 and sold to the L. E. White Redwood Lumber Company by May 1902. Part of the gigantic Spreckels sugar mill is visible behind the engine house. (Randolph Brant collection.)

PVCRR tank engine No. 9 takes on water at Salinas in 1923. No. 9, fabricated by Baldwin in July 1896, was built for the Spreckels Sugar Beet Company and serviced until 1914, when it was used for the Pajaro Valley Consolidated Railroad. Both entities were owned and controlled by the Spreckels family. (Randolph Brant collection.)

Abandoned along with all the other PVCRR locomotives, No. 4 sits at Spreckels under Southern Pacific ownership on September 23, 1930. At its peak, the PVCRR had over 32 miles of 3-foot-gauge trackage and 223 freight cars, but only 1 passenger car. More importantly, it earned a profit for its investors—Spreckels and its associates. (Randolph Brant collection.)

The one passenger car of the PVCRR dates from San Francisco's Ferries and Cliff House Railway's Park and Cliff steam lines, which connected with that company's cable car system at California and Central (now Presidio) Avenue. After PVCRR abandonment, the car rots away in an isolated sand dune. As late as 1909, the PVCRR offered six daily passenger Spreckels-Salinas round-trips and one daily Spreckels-Watsonville round-trip. (Randolph Brant collection.)

A close examination of the wooden Spreckels sugar mill shows, in the left front, the narrow-gauge tracks and engine facilities of the PVCRR. Southern Pacific standard-gauge tracks are in the foreground, and its freight cars are in the middle distance. With the subsequent construction of the brick mill, Spreckels could boast of having "the world's largest sugar factory." (Randolph Brant collection.)

The successor to the Watsonville sugar mill was this large brick edifice, constructed at the start of the 20th century and located south of Salinas at the town of Spreckels. In the foreground is the Salinas River Bridge of the PVCRR. This bridge collapsed twice—in 1914 from flooding and a few months after it was rebuilt, from the weight of a train, causing one fatality. (Randolph Brant collection.)

The Watsonville Transportation Company, designed largely as a competitor to the PVCRR, connected Watsonville with Port Watsonville, a distance of 6 miles. The line was a 6-foot-6-inch electric type. Here passenger motor No. 2, one of the two-car fleet, appears at Watsonville. (Randolph Brant collection.)

This early view depicts the original Port Watsonville Pier with a Watsonville Transportation Company passenger motor in the foreground. Designed to provide water access to San Francisco and other markets, the pier proved an economic liability, as it too often was the victim of the raging waters of the Pacific Ocean. (Randolph Brant collection.)

The Watsonville Transportation Company owned its own oceangoing steamship, the *F. A. Kilburn*, named for one of the firm's incorporators. It was operated as a produce packet between Monterey Bay and San Francisco. In 1910, the ship was sold by the company, which found it more economical to connect with existing freight lines. (Randolph Brant collection.)

to Del Monte

Start your vacation when you leave your home or office. Rest while you ride. Save time, money and nervous energy. Arrive there ready for play.

Special train service to Del Monte.

The speedy *Del Monte Express* leaving daily at 3 p.m. for the swift, interesting trip down the peninsula; arrives Del Monte 6:20 p.m. Special equipment to assure your comfort —observation parlor car, chair car and smoker in addition to long, smooth-riding coaches.

3 other trains daily with convenient departure and arrival times.

Visit Del Monte, Monterey, Pebble Beach, Pacific Grove, Carmel, Carmel Highlands and other charming resorts.

$6.00

roundtrip to Del Monte.

Tickets on sale any day until Sept. 30; good for 16 days.

Southern Pacific

Ferry Station   65 Geary Street   Third St. Station
Phone DAVENPORT 4000

The major promoter of the beauties and recreational wonders of Monterey and Pacific Grove was the Southern Pacific Railroad, whose line left the Coast Line for Pacific Grove at Castroville. In 1926, for $6 round-trip from San Francisco, one could visit the "charming resorts" of the Monterey Peninsula. Four daily trains, including the famous Del Monte, were at one's service. (Val Lupiz collection.)

During the late 1800s, the road engine of choice for the Southern Pacific was the 4-4-0, as shown at the Monterey depot pulling the Del Monte Express, a train that SP advertised as "The Fastest Passenger Flyer West of the Missouri River." This photograph was taken in 1898. (Art Lloyd photograph.)

In March 1949, Locomotive Historical Society excursionists enjoy rare trackage for the general public—namely, the Fort Ord military base loop, 5 miles north of Monterey. Famous for basic training, Fort Ord opened in 1917 and closed in 1994. (Art Lloyd photograph.)

Two-cylinder cross-compound engine No. 2923, built by the American Locomotive Company in 1898, pulls a series of heavyweight cars at Asilomar in July 1951. Within two years, No. 2923 will have rendezvoused with the scrapper. (Art Lloyd photograph.)

Extra No. 2375 arrives at Del Monte in March 1953 during an era of "pedestrian" traffic. From 1879 until 1924, the Southern Pacific operated "the Newport of the Western Continent," the Del Monte Hotel, which catered to the decorous and well-heeled elite of San Francisco. (Art Lloyd photograph.)

In March 1953, passenger extra No. 2373 stops at Castroville, the point where the branch to Monterey and Pacific Grove leaves the Coast Line. Castroville's unique claim to fame is the title of "Artichoke Capital of the World." Perhaps the lack of rail fans on the platform is because of a quick artichoke hunt. (Art Lloyd photograph.)

Train No. 78, southbound from San Francisco to Del Monte, thunders past a sided excursion train near Castroville in July 1951. When Monterey–San Francisco passenger train journeys ended with the 1971 advent of Amtrak, the Del Monte was the longest-operated name train in the country, with more than 80 years of service. (Art Lloyd photograph.)

No. 2912, one of 14 twelve-wheel engines built by the American Locomotive Company in 1895, leads an excursion train through the sand dunes at the U.S. Army's Fort Ord base on March 13, 1949. Today Fort Ord, located 115 miles south of San Francisco on the Monterey Peninsula, is best remembered as a training facility for basic combat and advanced infantry training. (Art Lloyd photograph.)

Near the Pacific Grove end of the Monterey Peninsula line was Lake Majella—a creation of the Southern Pacific marketing department, since it was in reality more of a pond than a lake. The former surrounding sand dunes and Lake Majella are today part of the golf course at Spanish Bay. For these Locomotive and Historical Society excursionists, the lake provides a pleasant halfway-point interlude in March 1949. (Art Lloyd photograph.)

At the time of this July 1951 photograph, excursion passenger service to Monterey under the banner of the Del Monte still had another 20 years of operation. Though the Monterey Peninsular trackage has been purchased by local governments, the Del Monte's revival is anything but certain. The money is not there yet, and so comparable scenes to this may never be repeated. (Art Lloyd photograph.)

Built to the economic requirements of its small population base, the Monterey and Pacific Grove (M&PG) was a single-track system with passing sidings. In 1905, the system was converted from the 3-foot-2-inch narrow gauge to standard gauge. Prior to the onslaught of automobiles, No. 18 (renumbered 3 in 1918) proceeds along Lighthouse Avenue in Pacific Grove in September 1907. (Randolph Brant collection.)

M&PG No. 5, originally constructed as an open car by the St. Louis Car Company in 1904 and rebuilt to an enclosed motor in 1918, stops in front of the Pacific Grove Methodist Church on Lighthouse at Seventeenth Street in September 1920. (Randolph Brant collection.)

The motorman of M&PG No. 3, an unmodified 1904 St. Louis Car Company California-style car—open end sections with an enclosed center—prepares to power the car around the bend off Lighthouse Avenue onto Pacific, near the beach and Municipal Wharf in Monterey, in September 1920. (Randolph Brant collection.)

The 34-foot-long M&PG No. 4 (pre-1918 No. 19) stops on the way to Pacific Grove's Southern Pacific depot at Monterey's Custom House on Alvarado Street in September 1920. Shortly before the 1905 conversion to standard gauge, the M&PG was taken over by Chicago's Byllesby Syndicate, the same group that would later run San Francisco's Market Street Railway from 1925 to 1938. (Randolph Brant collection.)

Looking at M&PG No. 5 in its 1907 configuration, one would not guess that it served the company as a single-truck horsecar for over 13 years, from 1891 to 1904. During 1904–1905, all 10 of the line's horsecars were rebuilt into electric cars. Besides adding motors and the appropriate electrical appliances, the cars were lengthened both in terms of platforms and passenger compartments, and double-trucked. They were all scrapped at the Del Monte carbarn in 1918. (Randolph Brant collection.)

In a sad accident reminiscent of the bygone era of the horse and buggy, the faithful steed met its match when it contested the latest of man's technological wonders—the electric streetcar—in 1908. No. 5's eclipse safety fender was not designed to be the last-minute salvation of horses. After some shop work at the Del Monte carbarn, No.5 would return for another decade of service. (Randolph Brant collection.)

M&PG No.19, outbound to Pacific Grove from the west gate of the Del Monte Country Club and Hotel, was the centerpiece of Monterey's Alvarado Street during the era of the horse in 1907. The wealthy and well-bred San Franciscans who are guests of the Del Monte would be horrified at the thought of a night at the Monterey Hotel. (Randolph Brant collection.)

The end of the M&PG nears as the multiplying automobiles are taking an increasing amount of street space and also ridership. The new congestion is making a shambles of the schedule for the single-track system. These factors, plus the reality that the entire plant soon needed to be rebuilt, caused the last M&PG streetcar to pull into the Del Monte carbarn on July 20, 1923. (Randolph Brant collection.)

The M&PG provided service locally, whereas the Southern Pacific was the regional connection. The historically important city of Monterey lies 118 miles south of San Francisco. With the arrival of the Southern Pacific, Monterey was conveniently connected to its important northern neighbor. A portion of the railroad's pre-1900 Monterey yard facilities and the city are depicted here. Note the wooden boxcars. (Randolph Brant collection.)

Monterey photographer C. W. J. Johnson has posed not only the engine crew of No. 10 (4-4-0), but also local Southern Pacific officials. After making prints, Johnson will return to hopefully sell a copy to each person. Thanks to Johnson's entrepreneurial skills, this classic, late-1890s portrait of Southern Pacific steam locomotive No. 10 exists today. (Randolph Brant collection.)

Nearing the Pacific Grove terminus of Southern Pacific's Monterey Peninsular line is engine No. 1438 with an express in tow from San Francisco, perhaps the Del Monte. During high season, more than six daily trains connected Pacific Grove and San Francisco. This train passes Monterey Bay's Grove Beach about 1910. (Randolph Brant collection.)

Four

STEAMSHIPS, STEAM ENGINES, AND ELECTRIC TRAINS
PACIFIC COAST RAILWAY

In 1876, San Luis Obispo was joined by rail with San Luis Obispo Bay. This operation would, in 1882, become part of the Pacific Coast Railway (PC), a 3-foot-gauge carrier. The company's founding entrepreneurs opted for narrow gauge to be able to purchase smaller, less costly locomotives and cars.

As long as the PC was isolated from the national rail network, being narrow gauge was not a liability. On May 5, 1894, the standard-gauge (4 feet 8.5 inches) Southern Pacific Railroad entered San Luis Obispo. Prior to the arrival of the Southern Pacific, the PC had a virtual monopoly on the area's commerce. With few exceptions, passengers and freight came and left the Central Coast via the Pacific Coast Railway and connecting steamships anchored at Harford's Wharf in San Luis Obispo Bay. The entrance of the Southern Pacific lessened this pattern. A problem the PC faced was that freight and passenger cars, because of the incompatibility of gauges, could not be through-routed to the nation. Southern Pacific, however, did not complete its Coast Line until 1901.

At its zenith, the PC stretched slightly more than 76 miles. San Luis Obispo was the line's economic hub. Besides San Luis Obispo and the port, the railway served Arroyo Grande, Nipomo, Santa Maria, Los Olivos, and way stations.

Despite competition, the PC continued, albeit as a largely marginal operation. Revenues and profits were buoyed by booms associated with the discovery of oil and gravel pits and in those years of exceptional agricultural harvests. In slack years such as 1913, only a single daily mixed train (passenger and freight) ran between the port and San Luis Obispo.

During the 1930s, several economic factors worked against the PC's survival. Added to railway competition was that of the truck and car. Paved highways now existed in ever-increasing mileage. The Great Depression also took its toll. As revenues declined, passenger service all but disappeared, freight schedules became infrequent, and trackage was reduced. Furthermore, the physical plant and rolling stock was not only becoming obsolete, but was worn out after years of deferred maintenance.

There was only one logical economic course: total abandonment. On December 20, 1941, the Pacific Coast Railway received government authorization to abandon its remaining trackage south of San Luis Obispo. The railway's last whistle sounded when on February 28, 1942, the 10 miles of line between San Luis Obispo and the port were sold to the Port San Luis Transportation Company. That firm ceased operations on October 29, 1942.

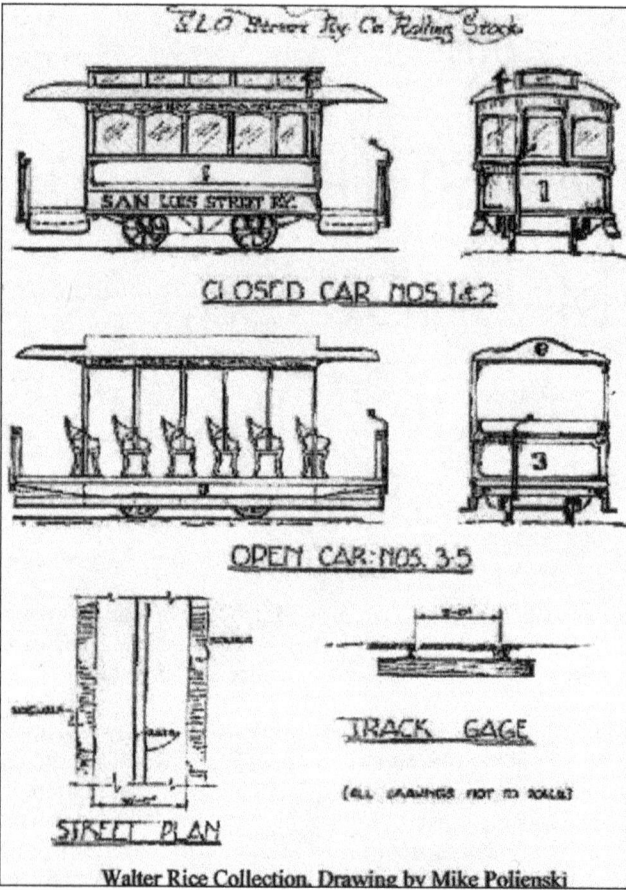

Serving the Pacific Coast Railway station on Higuera Street were the horsecars of the San Luis Street Railway. After the 1894 arrival of the Southern Pacific, most people walked to the more conveniently located station. (Mike Polienski drawing, Walter Rice collection.)

A Baldwin-built 2-8-0 will soon leave Los Olivos with the daily passenger train to San Luis Obispo. The 66-mile journey will take a little more than four hours. By 1909, direct service to Port Hartford from points south of San Luis Obispo had ended. (Randolph Brant collection.)

Pacific Coast Railway San Luis Obispo–Los Olivos passenger car 101 and baggage car 201 lay over in Los Olivos. The size of the train reflects the economic famine passenger service represented to the company during the 20th century. In 1938, No. 201 was sold to the White Pass and Yukon Railway, where it became baggage caboose No. 207. (Randolph Brant collection.)

In the 1930s, No. 109, built by Baldwin in 1906, and its train are on the spur the Pacific Coast Railway constructed from its mainline to the Southern Pacific depot after that railroad arrived in San Luis Obispo. This allowed for a direct transfer of passengers between the two railroads. (C. D. Whittaker photograph, Walter Rice collection.)

Economies were everywhere on the Pacific Coast Railway in the 1930s. To save money, the company name was no longer painted on engine and tender, illustrated by No. 105 as it switches freight in the Santa Maria Valley. Deferred maintenance was the official company policy. Passenger service had all but disappeared, and freight schedules were infrequent. (Walter Rice collection.)

The extra revenue brought by the Pacific Coast Railway's first rail fan outing, in October 1937, has resulted in a new paint job for No. 106. The engine builds up steam for the line's first such journey. A year later, No. 106 would be hit broadside by a gasoline tanker, wrecked, and scrapped, but for now it proudly displays the corporate title "Pacific Coast" on its tender. (Walter Rice collection.)

Built by Baldwin in 1904, No. 107 was retired for spare parts in 1935 as a result of the company's dire economic situation. Despite being derelict, it was an object of 1937 rail fan photography. The female rail fan is appropriately dressed for a shopping outing at San Francisco's Emporium. High-heeled shoes and the PC San Luis Obispo yard are incompatible. (Art Stump photograph, Walter Rice collection.)

No. 110 rests in the PC San Luis Obispo yard on October 20, 1940. It was acquired in May 1928 from the Nevada-California-Oregon, where it was served as that company's No. 10. It was the last PC locomotive to be under steam, as it was used to switch cars in 1942, after which it was stored for sale until 1948 and scrapped. (Will Whittaker photograph, Walter Rice collection.)

No. 111, pictured in San Luis Obispo in 1937, was No. 11 when acquired in May 1928 from the Nevada-California-Oregon. Nos. 110 and 111 had 44-inch drivers, whereas the rest of what had evolved into an all-Baldwin-built steam fleet had 36-inch drivers. No. 111 was sold to Hawaii's Oahu Railway in January 1942 and scrapped in 1946. (Randolph Brant collection.)

The Pacific Coast Railway's San Luis Obispo yards were located on Higuera Street just south of South Street, in an area that is now partially occupied by the Pacific Coast Center. Here the railway had complete maintenance and repair facilities; a roundhouse with turntable, as shown in 1941; a storage yard; and its San Luis Obispo depot. (Art Stump photograph, Walter Rice collection.)

74

As the 1930s advanced, the cost of switching an ever-decreasing number of freight cars with labor-intensive worn-out steam locomotives was becoming a serious economic burden for the PC. The solution was the 1936 purchase of a used Plymouth gasoline-powered switcher, No. 120, pictured in the San Luis Obispo yard in 1940. (Will Whittaker photograph, Walter Rice collection.)

In this rare view, Plymouth switcher No. 120 is seen on the Union Oil Company pier at Avila Beach on August 2, 1941. Built by the Fayte-Root-Heath Company of Plymouth, Ohio, No. 120 was sold to the Aaron Feher Company of Los Angeles in January 1942. (Art Alter photograph, Walter Rice collection.)

From the time of their 1928 purchase from the Florence and Cripple Creek, the 1500s were an important part the PC's boxcar fleet. This detailed photograph of No. 1516, one of the 1500–1518 series of cars, was taken at the San Luis Obispo yard on October 20, 1940. It shows the car's former number of 597. The 1500s were constructed by American Car and Foundry in 1900. (Will Whittaker photograph, Walter Rice collection.)

Combination car No. 106 was the last Pacific Coast Railway passenger car. Built by Carter Brothers of Newark, California, in 1887, it was rebuilt by the PC in 1909. The classic open-vestibule styling that characterized PC passenger equipment is shown at the San Luis Obispo yard on October 20, 1940. (Will Whittaker photograph, Walter Rice collection.)

In order to transport the anticipated large volumes of sugar beets and sugar economically, more than 20 miles of Santa Maria Valley trackage were electrified by 1909. The Pacific Coast San Luis Obispo shops created the E-1 for this service. The E-1 consisted of two General Electric 53-horsepower traction motors fitted to one of the trucks; the other truck and cab were from retired steam engine No. 2. Out of service since 1928, the E-1 awaits the scrapper in 1936. (Randolph Brant collection.)

A second product of the PC shops, the E-2 had four General Electric 53-horsepower traction motors—two per truck. Because of its extra power, the E-2 was the preferred engine for freight drags. In 1927, the local sugar factory was shut down. The E-2 sits in storage in this 1936 photograph. Both electric motors were scrapped in 1938. (Randolph Brant collection.)

From 1908 to 1912, passenger service on the electrified trackage between Santa Maria and Guadalupe was provided by the E-1 pulling combination car No. 300. Because of complaints by Santa Maria about the arrangement, the PC purchased a steel center-entrance interurban car from the Cincinnati Car Company—No. 3, which ran until 1928. (Randolph Brant collection.)

With a single-car fleet consisting of No. 3, the Pacific Coast Electric Railway provided up to six daily Santa Maria–Guadalupe round-trips connecting with Southern Pacific passenger trains at Guadalupe, where No. 3 is shown. Electric operations ceased in 1928; No. 3 soon lost its electrical equipment. In 1942, it was sold for scrap. (Randolph Brant collection.)

In 1912, the first year that No. 3 operated, 62,319 passengers were carried. By 1922, the number had dropped to a mere 3,547. The private automobile, as pictured in this c. 1924 view of the Main Street Santa Maria electric line, had become a major player. The PC was in a losing competitive battle with the truck and car. Paved highways now existed in ever-increasing mileage. (Walter Rice collection.)

At the end of its existence, the Pacific Coast Railway enjoyed a mild resurgence in passenger traffic as rail fans from both San Francisco and Los Angeles came for their "last ride." Here the first of such PC excursion trains consisting of four passenger cars, two flats, a caboose (site of photographer), and No. 3 (not shown) parallels U.S. 101 en route to Port San Luis on October 10, 1937. (Art Stump photograph, Walter Rice collection.)

This excursion, powered by No. 106, inches out on historic Harford's Wharf in San Luis Obispo Bay, where the PC once exchanged passengers and freight with connecting steamships. It is clear that the current management's policy toward passengers is nonexistent. Fans are on the top of the engine and tender. The photographer has positioned himself with many others on top of the caboose. (Art Stump photograph, Walter Rice collection.)

The PC crew is in the process of backing the consist off the wharf as part of a wye operation that will soon see the train back onto the wharf with streetcar No. 3 in the lead. Now the train is reversed, with engine 106 set to lead the trip back to San Luis Obispo. (Art Stump photograph, Walter Rice collection.)

The final excursion occurred on October 20, 1941. Locomotive 105 was substituted for 106 and flatcars for the passenger cars sold to the White Pass and Yukon Railway, with combination car No. 106 on the rear. In this image, the train is delayed at Hadley Tower, where the PC crossed the Southern Pacific, because it is Sunday and no tower man was on duty. The PC had not operated on Sundays in years. (Will Whittaker photograph, Walter Rice collection.)

Excitement is everywhere in Arroyo Grande. Locals mingle with rail fans from exotic places such as San Francisco. Abandonment south of San Luis Obispo would occur in two months. It is time to say goodbye to the Pacific Coast. (Will Whittaker photograph, Walter Rice collection.)

Acquired in 1928 by the Pacific Coast Railway, restored caboose No. 2 exists today as part of the California State Railroad Museum Collection in Sacramento. When photographed on May 2, 1942, three months after the PC had ceased, the scrapper appeared to be a more logical fate. (Art Lloyd photograph.)

Locomotive No. 105, built by Baldwin in 1904, powers the train that is pulling up the mainline tracks of the Pacific Coast Railway south of San Luis Obispo on June 20, 1942. The next year 105 would be sold for scrap. (Art Lloyd photograph.)

Acquired in May 1928 from the Nevada-California-Oregon Railway, No. 110 (built by Baldwin in 1910), coupled to car No. 106, is under steam perhaps for the last time on June 20, 1942. Despite World War II, it would be six years before 110 would be cut up for scrap. (Art Lloyd photograph.)

The Pacific Coast Railway's two-story South Street San Luis Obispo office and waiting room reflects the abandoned state of the company on May 2, 1942. Behind the waiting room was a freight house. It is interesting that the depot was not directly adjacent to mainline trackage. (Art Lloyd photograph.)

Railway boosters are everywhere at Southern Pacific's San Luis Obispo depot. Some sit on the PC excursion train, while others watch the engine of train No. 98, the Los Angles–bound Daylight, uncouple from its consist. During the age of steam, most coast-route trains had their steam engine

replaced in San Luis Obispo. Typically, the GS-class locomotives assigned to the Daylights ran without change. (Art Stump photograph, Walter Rice collection.)

$22.75

roundtrip to Los Angeles

good for 16 days. Season tickets good
until October 31, slightly more.

Swift, colorful, crowded miles; interests
new and different—lush valleys, mountains, interesting cities, 113 miles of your
journey along the blue Pacific—the 12-
hour trip of the non-stop

Daylight Limited

daily between Los Angeles and San
Francisco. Leaves at 7:45 a.m.; arrives at
7:45 p.m.

Rest and relax as you ride. Observation and club cars, coaches, Southern
Pacific diner and all day lunch car.

*Nine trains daily to Los Angeles in day
or night service.*

Southern Pacific

FERRY STATION	65 GEARY STREET	THIRD ST. STATION
	Phone DAVENPORT 4000	
	Oakland Offices:	
13TH & BROADWAY	1ST & BROADWAY STA.	16TH ST. STATION
Lakeside 1420	Oakland 7960	Lakeside 1630

"Rest and relax as you ride" on Southern Pacific's prestige Coast Line train, the Daylight Limited.
Perhaps you may want to enjoy the 1920s hallmark of a prestige train, the open-platform observation
car on the Limited's rear. On September 17, 1926, readers of the *San Francisco Call* were informed
of a round-trip to Los Angeles at $22.75. (Val Lupiz collection.)

Five

THE COAST LINE
CONNECTING THE CENTRAL COAST

Stretching from the "Citadel of the West," San Francisco, to its lesser cousin Los Angeles, the Southern Pacific's Coast Line nurtured and created wealth in the form of agriculture, minerals, and commerce. The Central Coast segment of the Coast Line began at Watsonville Junction, where the branch that served Santa Cruz and its environs left the mainline. The most famous train on this trackage was the Suntan Special. Until 1971, the Del Monte branched off south at Castroville, carrying passengers to Monterey and Pacific Grove.

The Coast Line hosted many famous trains. After its 1901 completion, for many years the Sunset Limited connected San Francisco and New Orleans. "The World's Most Beautiful Train" (and profitable too), the Daylight and its luxury all-sleeper overnight companion, the Lark, connected the line's terminal cities. Today Central Coast passenger service is provided by Amtrak with the Los Angeles–Seattle Coast Starlight and two Surfliners, whose northward trip ends at San Luis Obispo.

From Salinas to Santa Margarita, a distance of approximately 100 miles, ranching and agriculture dominated, giving rise to a growing wine industry at Paso Robles. The long-abandoned Coal Fields Railway connected McKay.

At Santa Margarita, the engineering spectacular begins. During the next four miles, 346 feet of elevation is gained until the summit is reached inside tunnel No. 6—the Summit Tunnel. Once the summit is obtained, the sound of the diesels' dynamic brakes prevail as the Coast Line begins an over-1,100-foot 13-mile descent to San Luis Obispo, with a maximum grade of 2.2 percent. This is accomplished by the line snaking down the slope of the Santa Lucia Mountains, reversing direction and then reversing again. The highlight is the world-famous Horseshoe Curve, where both ends of a train (from the middle) can be seen simultaneously. During the initial part of the descent, a series of tunnels bored through dormant volcanoes is encountered.

At San Luis Obispo, the economic contrast between steam and diesel is stark. During the steam era, Southern Pacific employment topped 500 to service locomotives, which had reached their range plus Cuesta Grade helpers. Diesel-powered locomotives, in part because of their greater range, are not as labor intensive.

Until 1941, connections were made here with the narrow-gauge Pacific Coast Railway. After San Luis Obispo, the Coast Line briefly touches the Pacific Ocean at Pismo Beach before entering Southern California territory. In 1996, the unimaginable occurred: the Southern Pacific vanished, swallowed up by the Union Pacific.

No. 3679, a 2-10-2 built by Baldwin in 1923, rests at the San Luis Obispo engine yard prior to being coupled to an outbound freight in August 1952. During the era of steam, San Luis Obispo was the point where Coast Line freights exchanged power, since the steamers' freight range was exhausted. (Art Laidlaw photograph.)

One of 651 ten-wheel locomotives on the Southern Pacific, No. 2344 prepares to depart San Luis Obispo to earn revenue for the railroad in 1953. Behind No. 2344 are important revenue sources—gondola cars that hauled sugar beets from field to refinery, until the emergence of artificial sweeteners significantly lessened the demand. (Art Laidlaw photograph.)

Released from the Baldwin Locomotive Works in 1921, No. 3713 is parked in 1950 just south of the Southern Pacific San Luis Obispo passenger depot, built in 1943. It is ready to enter Cuesta Grade helper service. A northbound Coast Line train needing No. 3713's extra power to reach Santa Margarita will soon arrive. (Art Laidlaw photograph.)

The classic Southern Pacific locomotive design, the cab-in-front articulated (two sets of drivers) engine, is represented here by No. 4253, built by Baldwin in 1942. No. 4253 is set for servicing, with a southbound freight drag in tow, at San Miguel on June 18, 1953. (Art Laidlaw photograph.)

The Coast Line mail and express business is heavy, judging from the fact that Southern Pacific is running multiple sections of train No. 72, the Los Angeles–bound Coast Mail. Powered by No. 4470 (former Texas and New Orleans No. 401), train 72 pauses at San Luis Obispo to pick up and discharge mail and express in June 1953. (Art Laidlaw photograph.)

Built for the Texas and New Orleans Railroad, No. 1809 and its brethren were transferred to the parent Southern Pacific in 1910. Pictured at rest in Salinas in 1954, No. 1809 awaits one of its final assignments, as diesel power is rapidly replacing what railroad management now regarded as uneconomical and obsolete: the steam locomotive. (Art Laidlaw photograph.)

A half-century after No. 2701 entered Southern Pacific service in 1904, the Baldwin Locomotive Works engine is still engaged in commerce, as evidenced by the freight it is leading from San Luis Obispo. Steam's replacement diesels have only a fraction of useful economic life. (Art Laidlaw photograph.)

No. 4415, stripped of its Daylight colors and streamlining "skirt," thunders north from San Luis Obispo in the 1950s, heading Coast Mail train No. 71. The train's few passengers would be carried on a 60-foot coach from the San Francisco–San Jose commute pool. (Art Laidlaw photograph.)

Two of Southern Pacific's trademark powerful cab-forward locomotives, Nos. 4176 and 4177, built by Baldwin in the late 1930s, work the San Luis Obispo yard in July 1953. With the cab in front, engine crews did not have to breathe noxious exhaust gases. (Art Laidlaw photograph.)

The all-around utility engines of the Southern Pacific during the steam era were the 2-8-0 consolidations. No. 2892, seen parked at the Palm Street crossing in San Luis Obispo in April 1950, and its 2-8-0 mates presented the largest quantity of engines on the SP roster. (Art Laidlaw photograph.)

The SP was the first railroad with 4-10-2 on its roster; therefore, locomotives such as 5008 were designated Southern Pacific–type engines. Built for mountainous freight service, No. 5008 will soon leave San Luis Obispo to scale Cuesta Grade on April 10, 1952. (Art Laidlaw photograph.)

With its 10 sixty-three-inch driving wheels pounding the rails at Carnadero in March 1953 and black smoke appropriately billowing, No. 5011 races at speed to the delight and enjoyment of onlookers. No. 5011 was a 4-10-2 built by the Schenectady works.

For Southern Pacific's Coast Line, the first half of the 1950s was a period of transition from steam power to that of diesel-electric. This change is classically illustrated by diesel unit No. 5238 coupled to steam No. 104 at Watsonville Junction on August 2, 1963. Soon No. 5238 and its kind would be victorious. (Art Lloyd photograph.)

During the late 1930s and 1940s, San Francisco was the playground city of the movie industry. Stars and executives would crowd the Pullman sleeper space of the Lark, Southern Pacific's luxury overnight San Francisco–Los Angeles train. Business was very good on the Coast Line in 1945, as one maximum-length Lark was insufficient to meet demand. Here the first section of the Lark nears Los Angeles after passing through the Central Coast. (Randolph Brant collection.)

Near Salinas, Southern Pacific cab-in-front articulated locomotive No. 4499 met its maker. Its boiler exploded because of a lack of water, but it did not derail. Fortunately, the site of the explosion was a field; parts of the locomotive were catapulted over a wide area. The local ladies have dressed for the occasion. (Randolph Brant collection.)

A long Southern Pacific freight train—the economic lifeblood of the company—starts to cross Stenner Trestle north of San Luis Obispo while ascending the Santa Lucia Mountains' Cuesta Grade. By this time in February 1984, most local rail business had been lost and long-through freight trains predominated. (Walter Rice photograph.)

The popularity of the Daylight, which soon made it the world's most profitable intercity train, resulted in management adding a second San Francisco–Los Angles Daylight train, the Noon Daylight. Northbound Morning Daylight train No. 99 is passed by Noon Daylight No. 96 near San Lucas in 1947. (Robert McVay photograph, Walter Rice collection.)

When it was time to celebrate America's bicentennial with a freedom train, the choice of locomotive was simple—Southern Pacific's General Service, popularly referred to as a Daylight locomotive, No. 4449. The new colors of red, white, and blue provided a striking combination. Together with the streamlined casting and side skirting that blended into the pilot, the locomotive's traditional beauty and speed was continued. No. 4449 is spending the night at San Luis Obispo in this April 26, 1977, image. (Walter Rice photograph.)

A steam engine is back in San Luis Obispo after an absence of more than 20 years. At one time, Southern Pacific employed over 500 workers whose duty was to provide care for steam locomotives. In April 1977, No. 4449 has its share of admirers. Soon it will head over Cuesta Grade and emerge at Santa Margarita from steam cleaning the roofs of Cuesta's tunnels. (Walter Rice photograph.)

When Southern Pacific executives began to formulate plans for a new streamlined train in the Depression year of 1935, the train was to be powered by the "most beautiful locomotive in the world." It was. Witness the May 1981 arrival in San Luis Obispo of restored No. 4449. (Richard Harris photograph, Walter Rice collection.)

Daylight locomotive No. 4449 spends the night in San Luis Obispo in 1981. When 4449 and its fellow General Service–class locomotives were assigned to the Daylight, Coast Starlight, or Lark, San Luis Obispo was but a very brief service stop. The powerful General Service locomotives' range allowed them to run the entire distance from San Francisco to Los Angeles—a world's distance record for a single locomotive. (Walter Rice photograph.)

The New Orleans World Fair Daylight lays over in San Luis Obispo on May 8, 1986. The scene is reminiscent of the late 1940s, before Southern Pacific downgraded its passenger service to the overnight all-coach San Francisco–Los Angeles Coast Starlight. (Walter Rice photograph.)

Racing past Mission San Miguel, Southern Pacific extra train 4449 is headed by a General Service locomotive of the same number on May 8, 1986. Until the railroad converted its passenger trains to diesel power in the mid-1950s, the General Service locomotives were as familiar to Californians as the palms, beaches, and orange groves they ran past. From the first in 1937, they were the world's most beautiful locomotives. (Walter Rice photograph.)

When the cry "4449 is coming" was heard, the San Luis Obispo rail fan community mobilized. Coauthor driver Walter Rice has achieved the optimal photographic motorcade prize; his car is directly parallel to 4449. The location is the back road between San Lucas and San Ardo. Soon Walter will step on the gas to move to the next planned stop. (Richard Harris photograph, Walter Rice collection.)

After a 16-year absence, overnight train service returned to the Coast Line on October 25, 1981, with the inaugural trip of Amtrak's Sprite of California. This short-lived train connected Sacramento and Los Angles. Here the first northbound Sprite welcomes coach and sleeping car passengers aboard in San Luis Obispo. (Walter Rice photograph.)

Want to go inside a dormant volcano? The 13 miles of track called Cuesta Grade that snake down the slope of the Santa Lucia Mountains, connecting Santa Margarita with San Luis Obispo, lead the Coast Line along the side of and into a series of dead volcanoes. This view from inside Tunnel No. 11's north (railroad east) portal is within one of the volcanic structures. The photographer knew how to read the handcar signaling. (Walter Rice photograph.)

With the 1971 Amtrak takeover of Southern Pacific passenger service, the Coast Line had but a single daily passenger train that ran from Los Angeles to Oakland four days a week and San Diego–Seattle tri-weekly. This evolved into daily Los Angeles–Seattle service under the name Coast Starlight. Train No. 11, the Los Angeles–bound Coast Starlight rounds Cuesta Grade's famous Horseshoe Curve in 1984. (Walter Rice photograph.)

Another distinctive feature of Cuesta Grade, Stenner Trestle carries the Coast Line over Stenner Creek. With the advent of Amtrak, Oakland replaced San Francisco in the Bay Area to allow (for the first time) direct Los Angeles–Seattle train service. This Coast Starlight, crossing Stenner Trestle in 1981, left Seattle's King Street station in the early morning the day before. (Walter Rice photograph.)

In order to increase productivity, Amtrak adopted the double-deck car design concept developed by the Santa Fe Railway. Called the Superliner, the train includes both coaches and sleepers on two levels, thus increasing carrying capacity. A long Superliner Coast Starlight with more than 400 passengers prepares to cross San Luis Obispo's Orcutt Road on April 23, 1994. (Walter Rice photograph.)

Amtrak's Los Angeles–bound Coast Starlight passes the long-out-of-service San Luis Obispo less-than-carload freight house in 1994. Today the railroad industry is enjoying record levels of freight traffic, but that traffic has shifted almost exclusively to major endpoint trains. Currently, the freight house is being restored as part of the San Luis Obispo Railroad Museum project. (Walter Rice photograph.)

Steam returned to San Luis Obispo for the May 5, 2004, centennial of the arrival (from the north) of the Southern Pacific. The Golden Gate Railroad Museum's No. 2472 was the featured steam locomotive pulling the celebration excursions. Here No. 2472 is at Paso Robles on its return to San Francisco on May 8, 1994. (Walter Rice photograph.)

In 1965, when the Southern Pacific discontinued the Lark and Starlight, San Luis Obispo's north county community of Paso Robles was left without passenger rail service. During the late 1990s, the passenger train returned when the Seattle–Los Angeles Coast Starlight began calling at Paso Robles. In honor of the return of passenger rail service, Paso Robles opened this handsome transportation center. (Walter Rice photograph.)

Until the 1990s, when Amtrak extended north to San Luis Obispo from Santa Barbara with its San Diegan (now Surfliner), Grover Beach never had a rail passenger stop; the closest was Oceano. Now two Surfliners stop at Grover Beach, and over 15,000 riders use the facility annually. This is but another sign of the Central Coast's long-term rail renaissance. (Walter Rice photograph.)

"Tracks Are Back" was the first marketing slogan for the then-new Amtrak in the early 1970s. For the Central Coast, this slogan was enhanced on November 17, 2005, as a second Surfliner train entered service between San Luis Obispo and Southern California. Train No. 798 climbs the Nipomo Mesa on its inaugural journey. (Jack Neville photograph.)

On October 9, 1940, readers of the *Call* were informed of the low $10.80 fare for San Francisco–Los Angeles round-trip. The Daylights—both Morning and Noon—now offered streamlined air-conditioned cars. The one-way trip took 9 hours and 45 minutes, down from the former 12-hour journey. Southern Pacific's management skills had made the Daylights the world's most profitable trains. (Val Lupiz collection.)

Snow in Santa Margarita! Even with 7 inches, Amtrak's Seattle–bound Coast Starlight is running on time. On that February day in 1984, the Coast Starlights were in essence the only surface transport between Santa Margarita and San Luis Obispo. The freeway was closed, but the Highway Patrol had forgotten about the old stagecoach road. The local rail fans had not. (Walter Rice photograph.)

During the 1960s, Southern Pacific management became anti–passenger train. Passenger trains, which regulatory authorities would not allow to be abandoned, were downgraded. The classic Daylight colors of orange, red, and black were replaced by a system-wide pedestrian silver with a scarlet band. The two parlor cars of the passing Daylights—Nos. 98 and 99—wear these new colors at East San Luis Obispo on June 1970. (Fred Matthews photograph.)

Train No. 98, the Morning Daylight, travels south in Price Canyon toward the Pacific Ocean at Pismo Beach in 1947. The Daylights—"the most beautiful train in the world," and America's most popular—connected Los Angeles and San Francisco on a nine-and-three-quarter-hour schedule. (Robert McVay photograph, Walter Rice collection.)

During the 1960s, the Southern Pacific Railroad regarded the Daylight as an economic pariah. The railroad downgraded its once-proud flagship. Costs were cut. Serves reduced. The traditional Daylight locomotive colors of orange, red, and black were replaced by an inexpensive gray with a scarlet nose, as illustrated in the San Luis Obispo August 1968 photograph. (Walter Rice photograph.)

Cabooses such as No. 47, being pushed in the San Luis Obispo yard by No. 2543 in August 1955, protected the rear of the train when stopped and provided crews with a shelter from which they could exit for switching. Their windows allowed the crew to inspect for problems such as shifting loads, and they created office space. (Art Laidlaw photograph.)

On May 1, 1971, the National Railroad Passenger Corporation (Amtrak), a quasi-public corporation, began operating Southern Pacific intercity passenger trains. Reflecting its new Amtrak ownership, with what critics referred to as the "pointless arrow," former Southern Pacific engine No. 6422, pulling the Coast Starlight (Seattle–Los Angeles) is being watered at San Luis Obispo, June 3, 1976. (Walter Rice photograph.)

The Coast Line's spectacular descent into San Luis Obispo is illustrated by this early-1900s Edward H. Mitchell postcard. Mitchell has taken license with this scene, as he has labeled it "Horseshoe Curve." The Horseshoe Curve is actually west of this location, and there are no tracks where the

train is running. The agricultural lands are now part of California Polytechnic State University, San Luis Obispo. (Walter Rice collection.)

April 10, 1915, was an exciting day to be a resident of the small Salinas Valley community of Gonzales. An even more exciting position would be that of a passenger on the first section passenger train, No. 10. Yes, the Coast Line was blocked. What caused the pileup has been lost to history; perhaps it was a broken rail. (Randolph Brant collection.)

In the 1970s, when the Seattle-Oakland segment of the Coast Starlight was running very late because of an accident or weather, Amtrak would run a replacement "stub train" to cover the Oakland–Los Angeles schedule. A southbound stub train, consisting of six short-haul Amfleet cars with over 300 passengers, has reached the end of double track at East San Lusi Obispo on St. Patrick's Day, 1978. (Walter Rice photograph.)

112

Two decades after the last of the Southern Pacific steam engines portrayed on these pages had their appointment with the scrapper, the nation celebrated its Bicentennial. Diesel-electric unit No. 3197 received a special Bicentennial paint scheme to mark this important milestone. The resplendent 3197 heads a freight train is at Santa Margarita, January 17, 1976. (Walter Rice photograph.)

No. 3679, a 1923 Baldwin 2-10-2 product, rests at the San Luis Obispo engine yard prior to being coupled to an outbound freight in August 1952. During the era of steam, San Luis Obispo was the point where Coast Line freights exchanged power, since the steamers' freight range was exhausted. (Art Laidlaw photograph.)

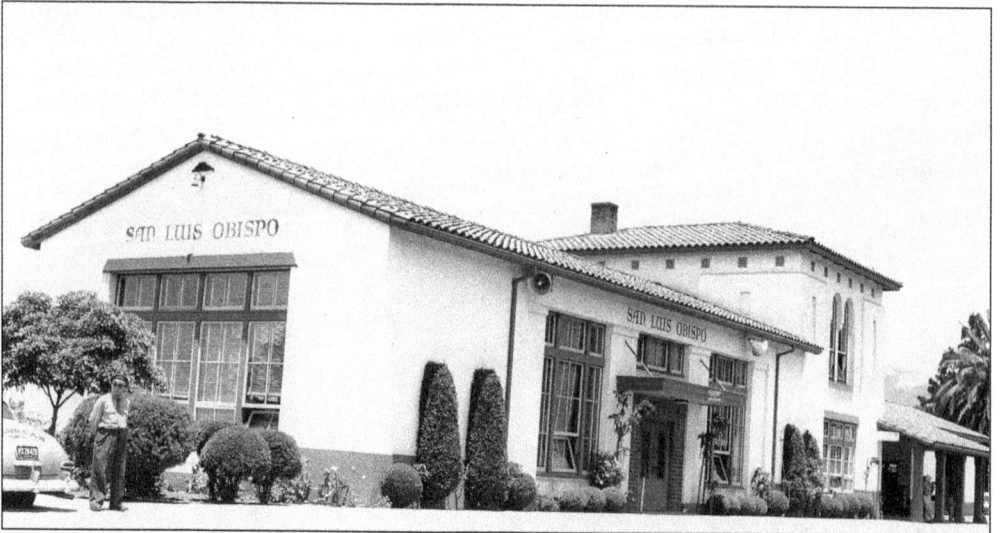

Opened by Southern Pacific during the war year of 1943, this peaceful June 1951 picture of the San Luis Obispo train station is deceptive by today's standards. During the fiscal year 2006, nearly 87,000 ticketed Amtrak passengers used the San Luis Obispo depot. Six daily trains enumerable Amtrak Thruway busses, city and regional busses, plus taxies service the facility. (Demoro Archives, Ken Meeker Collection.)

The classic Southern Pacific locomotive design, the cab-in-front articulated (two sets of drivers) engine, is represented here by No. 4253, built by Baldwin in 1942. No. 4253 is set for servicing, with a southbound freight drag in tow, at San Miguel on June 18, 1953. (Art Laidlaw photograph.)

Snaking down Cuesta Grade is a freight train with its white "SP" on a scarlet-painted nose—the symbol of the end of Southern Pacific's tenure on the Coast Line. In 1996, the corporate assets of the Southern Pacific were swallowed up by the Union Pacific, and armor yellow became the color of the day. (Walter Rice photograph.)

Built for the Texas and New Orleans Railroad, No. 1809 and its brethren were transferred to the parent Southern Pacific in 1910. Pictured at rest in Salinas in 1954, No. 1809 awaits one of its final assignments, as diesel power is rapidly replacing what railroad management now regarded as uneconomical and obsolete: the steam locomotive. (Art Laidlaw photograph.)

The Coast Line mail and express business is heavy, judging from the fact that Southern Pacific is running multiple sections of train No. 72, the Los Angeles–bound Coast Mail. Powered by No. 4470 (former Texas and New Orleans No. 401), train 72 pauses at San Luis Obispo to pick up and discharge mail and express in June 1953. (Art Laidlaw photograph.)

One of 651 ten-wheel locomotives on the Southern Pacific, No. 2344 prepares to depart San Luis Obispo to earn revenue for the railroad in 1953. Behind No. 2344 are important revenue sources—gondola cars that hauled sugar beets from field to refinery, until the emergence of artificial sweeteners significantly lessened the demand. (Art Laidlaw photograph.)

The first generation of diesel units on the Southern Pacific's prestigious Coast Line passenger trains proudly displayed the classic colors—black, orange, and red—of the General Service 4400-class steam locomotives. By this time, however, the Noon Daylight equipment had been reassigned to the overnight all-coach train, the Starlight. (Walter Rice collection.)

Consolidation No. 2918, an 1898 product of Schenectady, is at the west end of the San Luis Obispo yard in June 1952. From this point, the yard had a slight downward grade that allowed freight cars to be coasted into freight blocks. Dieselization was rapidly spreading on the Southern Pacific, and 2918 would soon pay the ultimate price: the wrecker's torch. (Art Laidlaw photograph.)

118

Acquired in early 1953 from the St. Louis Southwestern, where it served as No. 804, the 4-8-4 Southern Pacific No. 4476 sits at the San Luis Obispo engine facility in June of that year. Because of the relatively limited range of steam locomotives (compared to diesels) and its location halfway between Los Angeles and San Francisco, San Luis Obispo enjoyed considerable railroad employment. (Art Laidlaw photograph.)

The freight business must be good in December 1953 because consolidation No. 2592, Baldwin 1907, is powering an X2592 southbound (railroad east) from San Luis Obispo. During the steam and into the diesel era, many Southern Pacific freight trains were regularly scheduled. Extra trains were assigned "X" and the engine number. (Art Laidlaw photograph.)

Soon another freight train will arrive in San Luis Obispo from the south and will drop its exhausted power. No. 2837 will then couple to the consist to continue its northward (railroad west) trip, soon tackling the one major Coast Route obstacle: the Santa Margarita Hill and its 2.2-percent ruling grade. (Art Laidlaw photograph.)

No. 4380, in the middle of the San Luis Obispo freight yard, was part of a 1943 Baldwin order for 20 cab-forward locomotives. These were the last new steam locomotives purchased by Southern Pacific. The diesel age soon would be gaining momentum. Note how active the freight yard was in June 1953, largely as a result of local agricultural production. (Art Laidlaw photograph.)

Built by Baldwin in 1930, unstreamlined No. 4404 was part of the initial subclass of General Service 4-8-4 locomotives that for over 20 years drew SP's prime passenger assignments. In this image, however, No. 4404 hauls the Coast Mail, train No. 71, from San Luis Obispo. (Art Laidlaw photograph.)

Coast Mail train No. 71 stops at Serrano, the longest siding between San Luis Obispo and the summit of Cuesta grade, in 1953. The Santa Lucia Mountains are the backdrop. On January 7, 1955, steam operations on the Daylight, Lark, and Starlight would end; however, for another year the Coast Mail would be pulled intermittently by steam, making it the last scheduled Coast Line steam passenger train. (Art Laidlaw photograph.)

The Stone Canyon and Pacific Railroad built a 21.50 line east from the Southern Pacific Coast Line at McKay, north of Paso Robles, to the Canyon Consolidated Coal Company mines in Stone Canyon. The line opened in January 1909; in 1920, the California Coal Fields Railroad acquired it. (Randolph Brant collection.)

The long-forgotten Coal Fields Railway, the 1920 successor to the Stone Canyon and Pacific Railroad, continued to tap the coal fields of Coalinga and the vicinity. Engine No. 2288 was a former New York Central System consolidation. Evidence suggests that the Coal Fields Railway was abandoned by 1932. (Randolph Brant collection.)

North of Watsonville Junction at Chittenden (San Benito County), another long-forgotten feeder railroad to the Coast Line—the San Juan Pacific—provided revenues to the Southern Pacific. This 7.94 railroad line connected the Coast Line with a cement plant, but as shown, it also had connecting passenger service. Opened in 1907, it was sold in 1912. (Randolph Brant collection.)

The May 1912 successor to the San Juan Pacific was the California Central Railroad. The company's No. 5, former Ocean Shore No. 5, is pictured switching at San Juan. The railroad ceased operations in December 1937 and was legally abandoned in 1943. (Randolph Brant collection.)

The Southern Pacific is in transition, as steam is phased off the roster in favor of the economic savings associated with diesel power. Diesel unit No. 3238 has been attached to a steam excursion to facilitate switching at Watsonville Junction in 1953. (Art Lloyd photograph.)

It is a historical day at the San Luis Obispo train station. The last coach on the now Amtrak Daylight is the first piece of railway equipment assigned to the Coast Line to be painted Amtrack colors, July 8, 1972. The 48-seat, long-distance coach is a former Santa Fe that was built in 1953 by Budd. (Walter Rice photograph.)

SALINAS
RODEO
JULY 18, 19, 20 & 21

GO BY TRAIN to the *24th Annual California Rodeo* at Salinas, July 18, 19, 20 and 21. Southern Pacific offers special excursion fares and fast, convenient service. You can leave in the morning and return the same day, or stay longer, if you wish. Here are the

SPECIAL EXCURSION FARES

$2 ROUNDTRIP. Go July 18, 19, 20 or 21. Return the same or following day. $2.50 ROUNDTRIP. Leave July 18, 19 or 20. Return limit July 22.

The Rodeo Arena is a mile from the Southern Pacific station. Busses and taxis meet all trains.

GENERAL ADMISSION $1

Southern Pacific

For any other fares or passenger information, phone DOuglas 1255.
(Other railway business, DOuglas 1212.)

"Happy days" have yet to return for most Californians, as the impact of the Great Depression is everywhere in 1935. The Southern Pacific is facing the crisis by aggressively seeking out business. Its special excursion fares and extra train service from San Francisco to the 24th Annual California Rodeo at Salinas are but two examples of the positive policies of the company during this period of despair. (Val Lupiz collection.)

Disneyland has come to the Central Coast! Some of the original 1955 Disneyland Railway stock is being privately operated (not generally available to the public) at San Luis Obispo County's Santa Margarita Ranch, where it is known as the Pacific Coast Railroad. A 1927 Vulcan locomotive (2-4-0) pulls the 1955 Disneyland coaches past No. 1 (4-4-0), which is parked on Horeshead Spur, in 2006. (Karl Hovanitz photograph.)

BIBLIOGRAPHY

Best, Gerald. "The Story of the Pacific Coast Railway." *Western Railroader*. March 1965.

Dunscomb, Guy L. *A Century of Southern Pacific Steam Locomotives*. Modesto, CA: Self-published, 1967.

Fabing, H. W. "Watsonville Transportation Company." *Western Railroader*. November 1966.

Fickewirth, Alvin A. *California Railroads*. San Marino, CA: Golden West Books, 1992.

Fimrite, Ronald D. "The Yellow Jackets . . . Beautiful Locomotives." *Western Railroader*. May 1955.

Gibson, Jack. "Santa Cruz Cement Company." *Western Railroader*. April 1963.

Hanson, Erle. "Monterey & Pacific Grove." *Western Railroader*. September 1959.

McCaleb, Charles S. *Surf, Sand & Streetcars*. Glendale, CA: Interurbans, 1977.

Rice, Walter. "San Luis Obispo's Other Railroad: The Pacific Coast Railway." *San Luis Obispo County Journal*. February 2006.

———. "San Luis Street Railway." *San Luis Obispo County Journal*. November 2005.

Wagner, Jack R. *The Last Whistle*. Berkeley, CA: Howell North, 1974.

Visit us at
arcadiapublishing.com

....

www.ingramcontent.com/pod-product-compliance
Lightning Source LLC
Chambersburg PA
CBHW050543110426
42813CB00008B/2240